Quiet Spaces

The brf prayer and spirituality journal

W0007577

The Water of Life

Edited by Heather Fenton

Text copyright © BRF 2012
Authors retain copyright in their own work

Published by
The Bible Reading Fellowship
15 The Chambers
Abingdon, OX14 3FE
United Kingdom
Tel: +44 (0)1865 319700
Email: enquiries@brf.org.uk
Website: www.brf.org.uk
BRF is a Registered Charity

ISBN 978 1 84101 874 4
First published 2012
10 9 8 7 6 5 4 3 2 1 0

Acknowledgements
Scripture quotations taken from The Holy Bible, New International Version (Anglicised edition) copyright © 1973, 1978, 1984, 2011 by Biblica (formerly International Bible Society). Used by permission of Hodder & Stoughton Publishers, an Hachette UK company. All rights reserved. 'NIV' is a registered trade mark of Biblica (formerly International Bible Society). UK trademark number 1448790.

Scripture quotations taken from The Holy Bible, New International Version, copyright © 1973, 1978, 1984 by Biblica (formerly International Bible Society), are used by permission of Hodder & Stoughton, an Hachette UK company. All rights reserved. 'NIV' is a registered trademark of Biblica (formerly International Bible Society). UK trademark number 1448790.

Scripture quotations taken from The Holy Bible, Today's New International Version. Copyright © 2004 by Biblica (formerly International Bible Society), are used by permission of Hodder & Stoughton, an Hachette UK company. All rights reserved. 'TNIV' is a registered trademark of Biblica (formerly International Bible Society).

Scripture quotations taken from The New Revised Standard Version of the Bible, Anglicised Edition, copyright © 1989, 1995 by the Division of Christian Education of the National Council of the Churches of Christ in the USA, are used by permission. All rights reserved.

Scriptures quoted from the Good News Bible published by The Bible Societies/HarperCollins Publishers Ltd, UK © American Bible Society 1966, 1971, 1976, 1992, used with permission.

A catalogue record for this book is available from the British Library

Printed in the UK by Rainbow Press

VOLUME 24
Contents

The Editor writes.......................................4
Heather Fenton

The water of life 6
Thomas O'Loughlin

A gushing well 12
Katharine Smith

Searching for living water:
pilgrimage, wells and
sacred space... 18
Andrew Jones

Longing for living water 25
Naomi Starkey

My space 29

The waterless places:
desert and spirituality 30
Margaret Harvey

Make yourself a quiet corner 37

Hope for the downcast 40
Tony Horsfall

Margaret's space....................................44
Margaret Harvey

Prayers..47
Carol Jerman

My space 54

A poem about water.............................55

Water and prayer Celtic style.............56

A psalm for singing: Psalm 1.............58

Like a tree planted by the
waterside… 59
Heather Fenton

Embracing Dusty Detours 62
Lynne E. Chandler

My space 68

Jesus: Name above all Names...........69
Anne le Tissier

And at the end of the year… 76
Heather Fenton

The Water of Life

The Editor writes...

Heather Fenton is the Editor of *Quiet Spaces*.

Welcome to this issue of *Quiet Spaces*. I hope you will find some good things as we think about Jesus as the water of life.

Thomas O'Loughlin sets us off with his article 'The water of life', pointing out that 'we find water playing a central role in our imaging the interaction of God and us'. The story of the woman at the well in John 4 is the focus of the piece by Katharine Smith, and Andrew Jones enables us to explore the relationship between pilgrimage, holy wells and sacred space.

Naomi Starkey, my predecessor as editor of *Quiet Spaces*, has written a meditation on longing for living water. Isaiah writes of the desert as a place that God will transform into pools of water (41:18) and Margaret Harvey talks of the desert as becoming a place of meeting with God.

The writer of Psalm 42 begins with the words, 'As the deer pants for streams of water, so pants my soul for you, my God' (NIV), and Tony Horsfall focuses on facing depression, showing us that the psalmist feels like a deer running for its life, harried and exhausted by the chase and desperate for refreshment and safety.

I live in Wales and have an interest in Celtic spirituality. I have written a short article entitled 'Water and prayer Celtic style'. St David is sometimes known as 'Dewi Dŵr'—the Welsh word *dŵr* means 'water'—and so the article says something about David.

I have been editor of *Quiet Spaces* since 2009 and, as my time doing this comes to an end, I reflect on the past and look to the future during a period of a number changes in my own life. There is a time to look ahead and rejoice at what is to come, even if I know little of what it may hold. This is because at the end of all ends, there is Jesus. So I close with an article 'And at the end of the year...' together with an extract from a book recently published by BRF.

From the May–August 2013 issue *Quiet Spaces* will take a different form. It will continue to offer the reader ways of engaging deeply with God while providing a structure, similar to our Bible reading notes, that enables the reader to return to it regularly as a daily companion.

Each issue will contain material for four months of the year, presented in fortnightly sections. This material can be used in daily portions throughout the week or all in one sitting as a 'quiet day', perhaps at the weekend. Within each section there will be twelve elements comprising reflections inspired by different traditions, creative activities, liturgy, Bible reading and ideas for meditation.

Fortnightly themes will be explored in a range of different ways, allowing for different personalities and styles. The contributors will look at some of the classic writers on prayer and explore how we can learn from them, as well as using the Bible in prayer and building on the themes that *Quiet Spaces* has traditionally been so good at addressing. Creative ways of entering the themes and of responding to them will give readers the space to explore their innate spirituality and grow in their relationship with God our creator and redeemer.

My thanks to all of you who have been part of the journey. May you continue to grow in your knowledge of the one who is light, who is bread, who is water, who is all in all.

The water of life

author

Thomas O'Loughlin is the Professor of Historical Theology in the University of Nottingham and has written many books and articles, including contributions to previous issues of *Quiet Spaces*.

For anyone who lives in the shadow of Gulf Stream—that is, everyone in the British Isles—water is an ambiguous blessing. We know that we need it—it is essential for life—and when we think about it, we realise just how it affects so many other parts of life: washing, sanitation, sport, fun, gardening… and even transport and power. Using it just for the 'essentials' (drinking and washing) would make life far less pleasant: even if we do not fish or own a boat, just strolling near a lake in a park or seeing a 'water feature' in a garden enhances our experience. Strangely, it is always these 'additional' (some might say 'secondary') aspects of human needs that make life worth living: we need water for life, but life

without beauty, pleasure and fun would be very difficult! Yet we can easily have too much of this good thing. Not just occasional flooding or fatal accidents, but the dreary darkness of wintry clouds, and rain seeping into us, can depress us, and mould and damp, apart from costing us a fortune, call to mind squalor and decay. Water, in all its aspects, is always close to us. It is little to be wondered at, therefore, that, since we think and speak of the Great Mystery in terms of the creation surrounding us, we find water playing a central role in our imagining the interaction between God and us.

In Matthew's Gospel, the image Jesus uses as an expression of the generosity of the Father's love is that he sends rain on the righteous and the unrighteous. This is unlike our loving, which favours those of whom we approve (equalling 'the righteous'), or, at least, tends to disfavour those of whom we disapprove (equalling 'the unrighteous'). 'But I say to you, love your enemies and pray for those who persecute you, so that you may be children of your Father in heaven; for he makes his sun rise on the evil and on the good, and sends rain on the righteous and on the unrighteous' (Matthew 5:44−45, NRSV). The ambiguity of water is also seen in the story of the house built on sand: it was the rain, floods and wind that threw it down (7:27). Then again,

Water is an ambiguous blessing, essential for life…

> Water, that basic life need, can carry within our understanding the relationship of God to our existence

it is the basic act of giving someone in need a cup of water that can be the acid test of discipleship: 'And whoever gives even a cup of cold water to one of these little ones in the name of a disciple—truly I tell you, none of these shall not lose their reward' (10:42). Water, that basic life need, can carry within our understanding the relationship of God to our existence: to the woman at the well in Samaria who offers Jesus a drink of water, he replies, 'Everyone who drinks of this water will be thirsty again, but those who drink of the water that I will give them will never be thirsty. The water that I will give will become in them a spring of water gushing up to eternal life' (John 4:13–14). Just as somehow involvement in water is a key to this life, involvement

with the Christ is a key to eternal life.

When one teaches New Testament, one of the most important aspects of the course is to make sure that the students recognise just how different life, and assumptions about life, were in the past from those of our time. Failure to realise these differences is the root problem in biblical fundamentalism. So it is nice occasionally to come across something like the importance of water with its value and symbolism unchanged. You and I need water as much as Jesus or

I was given a questionnaire with a whole sequence of tick-box questions about beliefs

that unnamed woman at Jacob's well; we fear rain and flood just as we need fresh water for crops and for washing and for fun. So how can water speak to our religious imaginations?

Water and thanksgiving

To recognise ourselves as dependent creatures is at the core of Christian identity: my existence is not absolute but belongs within the creation—and the creation exists in its dependence on God. Put another way, creation is gift, pure gift, and to be valued as a gift, and the first religious act is thankfulness for that gift. Water—that most common element—is a gift and as such is something for which I should praise God. Recently, I was given a questionnaire with a whole sequence of tick-box questions about beliefs. It was a quite serious affair intended to provide scientific-looking data on religious belief, and on the basis of the answers one could be classified as a Christian, a theist or an atheist. It would have been far more informative, if not so quantifiable into neat cohorts, to ask, 'Can you imagine water as a gift?' and 'If it is a gift, does it make sense to you to be thankful for it?' If we can answer 'yes' to these questions, then we are well on the way towards a life of faith, although we might not even know the answers to some of the more detailed questions about Christianity that were on the questionnaire I saw. By contrast, if one were to answer 'no' to imagining water as a gift and something for which to offer thanks, then even if one were to tick a box marked 'yes' beside the Nicene Creed every morning, one would be de facto lining up in the atheist camp.

> Creation
> is gift,
> pure gift,
> to be valued
> as a gift

Only when I can imagine something as basic as water as a gift can I set out to imagine all the rest of life's good things as God's gifts and then imagine still more that there are gifts beyond this life: the life of God in Christ Jesus, forgiveness, and the gift of life that wells up to eternal life. It is the basic faith that enables me to recognise/imagine/think of a glass of water as a fragment of God's generosity that is the work of the Spirit within me—and it is the Spirit that then gives me voice to utter thanks. How appropriate that the Spirit has been so often imagined as being like rain and dew seeping into us and giving us life.

Water and need

If I can imagine water as God's gift and utter thanks for it, as an act of basic faith, I recognise also that we live in communities. Discipleship cannot be separated from the communities that we live within and impinge upon, and today's global economy means commitments to the global community.

The significance of Christian faith is transformed and it becomes transforming

---

The questionnaire I was asked to fill in assumed that religion, faith or belief was primarily, indeed almost exclusively, a matter of mental opinions. The questioners assumed that knowing beliefs was equivalent to canvassing historians as to which of several explanations of a set of phenomena they favoured. True, Western Christians have a long history of treating religion (traditionally labelled 'faith') as distinct from actual involvement with others ('works'), which was seen as simply some sort of secondary consequence of mental acts. I cannot be separated from my actions, and my imagination cannot be immune from the realities around me. In 'religious matters' one might try to distinguish 'faith' from 'works', but could one do this in the love of a partner or family or friends? When I grasp that water is God's gift, I must reflect that it is a need of my community and that all the individuals who make up the community need it as much as I do myself. I am suddenly drawn from what could become just another pious reverie into the world of justice: to be thankful to God for a gift involves commitment from me to the way I act as a human being towards other human beings. I cannot adequately imagine my relationship with God unless my

... a glass of water as a fragment of God's generosity

Aid to the development is, thereby, a basic demand of faith rather than an accidental consequence. Once one begins to imagine the world in this way, the significance of Christian faith is transformed and it becomes transforming. The world of that questionnaire is somehow as safe and cosy as its tick-boxes are irrelevant. When we can hold a glass of water and, looking at it, imagine not only a new set of earthly relationships but a relationship that reaches beyond the creation, then we are on path towards real faith.

relationships with others are also involved. Matthew explains this link between imagination and action quite bluntly when he reports the following statement of Jesus: 'Not everyone who says to me, "Lord, Lord," will enter the kingdom of heaven, but only the one who does the will of my Father in heaven' (7:21).

Now my recognition that my glass of water is a gift has some wide-ranging implications. Can I be genuine in thanksgiving and simply ignore the extent to which I can assist others to have the gift I myself value?

Blessed are you, Lord, God of all creation,

Through your goodness we have water which slakes our thirst and sustains our life,

And blessed are you for your Son who gives us the living water that becomes in us a spring of water welling up to eternal life. Amen

A gushing well

Jesus answered 'Everyone who drinks of this water will be thirsty again, but those who drink of the water that I will give them will never be thirsty. The water that I will give will become in them a spring of water gushing up to eternal life.'
JOHN 4:13–14 (NRSV)

author

Katharine Smith is the author of *Angels in the Wilderness: Hope and healing in depression* (Redemptorist Publications, 2010). She is also a Lay Reader at the parish church of St Andrew's, Taunton.

It may not seem to us at first that we can have much in common with a Samaritan woman who lived 2000 years ago in a culture very different from our own. It may not seem possible for us to share anything of what she experiences when she encounters Jesus at Jacob's well in the heat of the midday sun. In a moment we will walk alongside her to find out what we do share as God's children in his created world. We'll join her on the dry, hot and dusty track that runs between her village and Jacob's well, the only source of water for her and all who live in that village.

But first, let's think about the well and other ways in which water was collected and stored by the people of these New Testament times and also about how water is used as a symbol in biblical writings—a symbol that may well resonate with us across the centuries.

In many communities in New Testament times a well might be dug into the ground some distance from the dwelling places. It would gather water by infiltration from the soil around it and water jars would then be lowered into the well to collect the water. Other communities might use a cistern that simply stored water, which would quickly become stale and stagnant. During the rainy season, though, fresh, clean, 'living' water might be collected from streams and rivers flowing nearby. The word 'living' is used to describe fresh, moving, flowing water. It's also the word used by Jesus when he talks about the 'living water' of eternal life, which he will give to all who ask.

The biblical symbolism of water in both Hebrew scriptures and Christian writing is also very important as we consider this story. For example, in Jewish law water is used in various rituals as a symbol for purification. It's also used as a powerful metaphor for, among other things: the knowledge of

Our own deep longing for spiritual cleansing and renewal

God ('They will not hurt or destroy on all my holy mountain; for the earth will be full of the knowledge of the Lord as the waters cover the sea', Isaiah 11:9); salvation ('With joy you will draw water from the wells of salvation', 12:3) and, perhaps most importantly for us as we read this story, God's Holy Spirit ('For I will pour water on the thirsty land, and streams on the dry ground; I will pour my spirit upon your descendants, and my blessing on your offspring', 44:3).

So as we prepare to walk, unseen, beside the Samaritan woman, let's be aware of our own deep longing for spiritual cleansing and renewal, a deep thirst that we know only God can satisfy. We draw closer to this woman as she sets out from her village to fetch much-needed water. She walks alone, carrying a water jar which, even when empty, weighs her down and slows her steps. Coming back, it will be worse and the journey will seem longer and even more tiring.

Used to having water on tap, available at any time in any season and in limitless quantities, we have no use for wells and water jars. But maybe we do know what it is to walk through life carrying a heavy load on our shoulders, a weight that holds us back and wears us out with its persistent demands on our energy and strength.

Maybe it's depression, the illness that pushes down on us so that our whole being feels crushed; maybe it's a life-threatening illness, redundancy, financial insecurity, bereavement. A great many things in life can be hard to bear and perhaps too often we lose sight of joy, happiness, love and peace.

And, like the Samaritan woman beside us, we know tomorrow will be the same, and the next day and the day after that. What could happen to change this wearing daily pattern?

She walks alone, this woman of Samaria. Her lifestyle past and present has separated her from other village women. She's not welcome in their fellowship and, while they might tolerate her presence on this daily walk for water, she seeks to avoid their company. She's had enough of the staring, the disapproving looks, the whispering behind hands held up to mouths. She's given up on ever finding someone who tries to understand how and why she is where she is today.

Perhaps we too have felt isolated, an embarrassment to so-called friends who now cross the road to avoid having to speak to us. We may have heard in-sensitive remarks from people who don't understand us or our circumstances. Maybe we've been all too well aware of the fear of others that somehow our tragedy or unhappiness threatens them when they are comfortable.

Still quite a distance from the well, our companion sees a solitary man sitting on the well as if he is waiting for her. We sense her sudden tension and fear. It's happened to her before. Men who know that if she is coming to the well at this time of day, she's vulnerable, an outcast, maybe used to being assaulted or free with sexual favours. Men like that will take what they think they can get and who would care?

Carrying a water jar which, even when empty, weighs her down and slows her steps

It may not be a physical threat we fear from others but it might be something as painful and difficult to evade: the insensitive remarks, the judgmental criticism or even the failure to recognise that something is amiss. We steel ourselves for the unexpected, and somehow that defensive barrier never really comes down. We get trapped behind our own security bars.

We are now close enough to the well for our friend (and somehow we have come to think of her as our friend) to know that the man apparently waiting for her is a stranger, no one she recognises, and moreover he is a Jew. A fresh wave of tension breaks over her because the enmity between Jew and Samaritan is deep-rooted and sometimes bitter.

We, of course, know who it is sitting, waiting. We know it's Jesus and that the woman beside us will be transformed by him. Perhaps we too are aware of feelings of tension and apprehension. It's one thing to believe in Jesus, to learn about him and to try to walk in his way but actually standing in front of him, even if unseen, will surely be a completely different experience for us. We can only wait and see.

He speaks, holding his hand out in a gesture of friendship. 'Give me a drink,' he says. Nothing more, yet we have the strangest feeling that he has seen us, invisible to the woman from the village but already known to him. From now on we are part of this encounter, no longer bystanders watching a drama unfold before us.

The woman questions him, 'How is it that you, a Jew, ask a drink of me, a woman of Samaria?'

How can we relate to each other like this when so much lies between us? We too are aware of all that lies between us and Jesus: the loads we're carrying like jars filled to the brim with stale and stagnant water; the self-loathing and shame that keep our heads bowed;

The Water of Life **15**

the half-truths and self-deception that compromise our integrity. We feel we have nothing to give Jesus that isn't dirty and polluted.

Our self-absorption is pierced as Jesus speaks again and once again we have that unnerving sense that he is speaking to us as well: 'If you knew the gift of God, and who it is that is saying to you, "Give me a drink," you would have asked him and he would have given you living water.'

'Living water': water clean and clear; water flowing swiftly; water cooling, refreshing, cleansing, life-giving; streams, brooks, rivers, waterfalls, always on the move, never resting, the energy of life itself.

The words and images wash over us and we feel the beginning of something new in our hearts and minds. A sudden hope tells us that things could be different. We don't have to be held back in that stagnant water we've been stuck in for so long.

Now Jesus is saying to her, and to us—hidden from her view but not from his—'Everyone who drinks of this water will be thirsty again, but those who drink of the water that I will give them will never be thirsty. The water that I will give will become in them a spring of water gushing up to eternal life.'

'Water gushing up to eternal life'— the thought of the wonderful energy of 'gushing up' excites us. It reaches into the deepest places of our hearts and clears a way through all the obstacles our own defences have built to keep at bay the risk of being hurt, of failing or of feeling pain in any form.

Jesus reaches through it all, knows it all, understands it all, forgives and heals it all.

Why would we not want to receive that sort of water of life into ourselves? Like the woman of Samaria, we want to ask, 'Sir, give me this water, so that I may never be thirsty or have to keep coming here to draw water.'

She and Jesus continue their conversation but we will leave them at this point and return to today, to the here and now. The Samaritan woman will have to continue going to the well each day but Jesus has transformed her

'Water gushing up to eternal life'

isolation, her loneliness, her sense of shame. He has restored her to fellowship in her own community as she brings them also to meet Jesus, the Messiah.

We too will continue with our daily lives, still carrying some heavy burdens. Perhaps we too have in some way been changed, healed and refreshed by encountering Jesus at Jacob's well. Perhaps our feelings of being isolated and lonely have been lifted. Perhaps we feel more connected with the people around us and able to take our place among them. Perhaps we also will bring people with us to meet Jesus, the Messiah.

Water is needed to preserve life in all living things, and without it the earth would surely once again be 'a formless void' (Genesis 1:2) with no life in it. We need the gift of God's Holy Spirit to preserve our souls. We need to know that we have this living water within us 'gushing up to eternal life', enabling us to experience life as God meant it to be—life in all its abundance. Once we truly recognise this need and longing within us, we will open up our hearts and minds to receive the gift of God's

Spirit within us. And once we have received God's Spirit, it will never leave us. It will always be there, cleansing, renewing, refreshing and strengthening us. Its ever-flowing energy will bring us joy in even the most difficult and painful times—a joy, a peace and love that this world can never offer.

Prayer

Lord Jesus, you offered the gift of living water to the woman at the well.

You offered her living water, gushing up to eternal life.

You brought down barriers dividing people from one another and from you.

We pray that you will give to us that same living water.

Forgive us and cleanse us from all the things that separate us from you.

And whenever we feel tired, worn out and burdened,

Let us know once more the energy of that living water,

And the joy and peace that are also gifts of your Spirit. Amen

ANDREW JONES

Searching for living water:

pilgrims, wells and sacred space

author

Andrew Jones is an Archdeacon in the Church in Wales. He has written *Pilgrimage* (BRF, 2011) and *Every Pilgrim's Guide to Celtic Britain and Ireland* (Canterbury Press, 2002).

My interest in the relationship between pilgrimage, holy wells and sacred space began over 30 years ago when I was a student in Jerusalem. A group of us had planned an outing to Nablus, one of the largest cities on the West Bank, situated quite close to Mount Gerizim—the mountain that Samaritans believe to be holy in exactly the same way as Jews believe Mount Zion to be holy. To this day, quite close to Nablus stands one of the very few surviving Samaritan synagogues, and plans had been made for us to meet one of the Samaritan leaders who was to show us the *Samaritan Book*. On arrival, the Samaritan priest claimed that this was the oldest book in the world, written almost 4000 years ago, only 13 years after the death of Moses. Naturally, he also claimed that it contained the earliest version of the Pentateuch written by Abishua, the son of Phineas, on the skin of a sacrificed lamb. The Samaritan Bible comprises only the Pentateuch and so this was a crucial book for them. As we bade the priest farewell he pointed us in the direction of the nearby Jacob's Well. This was to have a much more lasting impression on me than the book that we saw but could not handle!

On our arrival at the well we read the opening section of John's Gospel, chapter 4, that tells the story of the encounter between the Samaritan woman and Jesus on this very spot. It was there that a certain penny dropped for me—that there was an exciting and significant connection between what we were at that particular time (pilgrims), where we were physically (a well) and the more general context of that whole land (sacred space). Over the years I have dipped into that experience on several occasions, not least because I

have felt since then that the connection between these three things has always been and continues to be very crucial.

A great deal has been written about the significance of holy places and sacred space and their significant role in people's journeys of faith. Interestingly, writers differ in their definition of 'place' and 'space' and these various attempts at defining reveal quite significant facets of the actual destinations. However we define them, both the concept and the experience of pilgrimage, whether in a historical or contemporary context, would make little sense without 'place' and 'space'. The idea of travelling alone or in a group to a particular holy place serves as a living metaphor against which pilgrims are able to retrace their very physical human journey of life. This is what is meant when we speak about the relationship between the journey of the heart and the journey of life—or the inner and the outer journey. The act of pilgrimage affords the pilgrim with the opportunity to reflect on his or her life while travelling and so, by pausing at various holy places, the pilgrim can call to mind particular memories or significant stages in life.

Of course, none of this is entirely new. Indeed, throughout the biblical narrative, 'travelling' is constantly a significant experience. Over and over again we read about key people in that narrative making spiritual journeys to particular places, either in response to a direct divine instruction (Abraham) or as an opportunity to encounter and worship God (the Magi). One of the most significant places of such encounter in the Bible is the desert. This is the place where the Bible records countless experiences of spiritual renewal and human purification. It was in the desert that Moses received the Torah; it was in the desert that Elijah discovered refuge; it was in the desert that John the Baptist proclaimed the need for a national repentance; it was in the desert that

Jesus renewed in a most radical way his own covenant with the Father.

By the third century, Christian men and women continued to seek God in the desert and in wilderness places, at the edge of all existence. Eventually these people were to travel westwards as pilgrims—even to Britain and Ireland—to the edge of the then known world. It is no coincidence that there are places of ancient origin both in Wales and Ireland known to this day as *Dyserth* (Welsh) and *Diseart* (Irish). These places originate precisely in the Eastern desert experience of seeking God 'out there'. An exciting exploration that occupies much of my own energy nowadays

is the careful study of some of the early Christian Celtic settlements that perpetuated this search for the 'edge'. The founders of such settlements were actually doing none other than imitating the biblical and very early Christian tradition of seeking God in places of solitude and wilderness alike.

As a modern-day pilgrim as well as a pilgrimage leader, something quite extraordinary has struck me in recent years. I have noticed that so many holy places that attract pilgrims have a significantly crucial common factor, namely, that they contain two places. This is where I distinguish between 'holy place' and 'sacred space'—the former being the more generic and the latter the more particular within any given destination. Let me explain: in Glendalough, for example, the holy place is centred around the medieval so-called Cathedral City—a place of popular pilgrimage—but a little distance away

It was in the desert
that Elijah
discovered refuge

Thinkstockphotos

near the upper lake is the sacred space known as St Kevin's Cell. Similarly on Iona, the original community gathered around a large church and monastery, and this became a holy place, but at some distance away is St Columba's Cell, a sacred space near a well. In Wales' Clynnog Fawr, the holy place is the monastery but the related sacred space is further away near a well in Pistyll: St Beuno's sacred space. In Oxford, St Frideswide established her community in the area around what is now Christ Church Cathedral but her sacred space was along the river Thames in Binsey, where there is a well. It is as if Kevin, Columba, Beuno and Frideswide, once they had established their communities in churches and monasteries, which would eventually become holy places for future pilgrims, then went in search of the 'edge' in order to encounter God at an even deeper level. Significantly these places of deeper encounter were usually to be found near a well and the well became the sacred space close to the holy place.

So, not two destinations but one—a place and a space—reflect a much older Christian practice of people searching diligently and constantly for depth of encounter and of renewal. By journeying to these places, contemporary pilgrims

> That source of life is only reached by descending into the depths of a deep dark shaft

continue to share the inheritance of what people like Paul of Thebes, Anthony of Egypt and Pachomius experienced in the desert of third- and fourth-century Palestine and Egypt. Theirs was an extraordinary experiment of a spiritual search for a deeper and a more authentic communion with God. These were early Christian men and women who were constantly travelling deeper and deeper into the wilderness of life's margins in order to seek a radical experience of the God who is always at the edge of all things.

It is of course no coincidence that in almost all of these pilgrimage destinations of 'holy place' and 'sacred space', there is a well that actually survives to this day. These holy wells seem to attract pilgrims like nothing

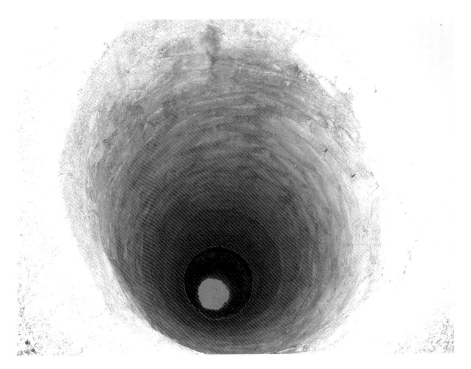

else and continue to capture the contemporary imagination. Christian and even pre-Christian legends, practices, beliefs and stories abound wherever there is a holy well. It is interesting also that those who specialise in the study of holy wells feel able to categorise them according to the traditions that surround the individual wells. There are saints' wells, pin wells, rag wells, healing wells and even wishing wells. But for me such categorisation raises certain contrived risks and difficulties. To my mind all so-called holy wells share an essential unity, and type categorisations overlap. Such overlapping strongly suggests to me the existence of an original well-cult, and that it is the cult that varies and should be categorised, and not the physical well itself. A well is a well wherever it is—a simple and basic source of life. If such physical wells stand in or close to a holy place, then the well is the sacred place to which men and women originally came in order to discover a deeper and more authentic encounter with God. The well served to sustain and nourish these people. Gradually, and admittedly quite possibly very early in the history of particular religious communities in these holy places, various cultic traditions grew and developed around the actual well, and this meant that it could legitimately be known as a holy well.

> ... to discover a deeper and more authentic encounter with God

In a Christian context, wells that are found on traditional pilgrimage routes almost certainly suggest that they would have been used for baptism, the renewal of baptismal vows, healing, places of physical refreshment or even merely comfort stops en route! However, in the ancient Celtic tradition the pilgrim was presented with an interesting paradox at these holy wells. The Celts revered their wells with particular devotion and respect as very sacred spaces primarily because they were sources of water—that vital (literally, *vita* being the Latin word for 'life') cradle and assurance of life itself. Yet, and here's the paradox, that source of life is only reached by descending into the depths of a deep dark shaft.

Times haven't changed! As contemporary pilgrims pause at those holy wells, hallowed by generations of people, we too are offered an opportunity to reflect on some of the deeper and possibly darker moments of our own lives. It is often in those particular pauses—as it was for Kevin, Columba, Beuno and Frideswide in their particular pausing moments on the edge—that we too are able to draw living water from those darker depths. It was, after all, in his wrestling with God at the waters of Jabbok that Jacob discovered a refreshed and renewed determination—so much so that he even changed his name to Israel (Genesis 32:22–32). In the actual wrestle Jacob was injured or disabled or scarred, but his strength remained firmly in what possibly became an enduring limp as a result of the wrestling. Today, we continue to visit these holy places, sacred spaces and wells and, like Jacob, we too may find ourselves wrestling with memories of times of injury or disability or scars. But as the waters of Jabbok reassured Jacob, so too the living waters of our holy wells will reassure us and strengthen us as pilgrims to keep travelling towards the real edge of all authentic existence, God.

Longing for living water

'My soul thirsts for God, for the living God...' (Psalm 42:2, NIV).

author

Naomi Starkey is a commissioning editor for BRF and a former editor of *Quiet Spaces*. She has previously written *Pilgrims to the Manger*, BRF's Advent book for 2010, and *Good Enough Mother* (2009) and *The Recovery of Love* (2012). See www.brfonline.org.uk for more information.

Are you thirsty?

I am.

The ground is dry and deeply cracked; the sun is high and hot and, as we sit, we cast no shadows on the cracked, dry ground. As far as we can see, the land is dry and brown. Look north, south, east and west and you will see nothing but brown.

This is a desert place.

You asked how long we have been here. I don't know exactly but if I think hard I remember somewhere else: a green valley, where there were shadows, leaves shifting in sunlight, a stream that brimmed its banks. If I think hard, I can picture us walking there together.

I remember that it was good.

You ask how we came to be here. I can't be sure, exactly, but when I think about it, it puzzles me. I didn't think we had travelled so far, so fast. Somehow we managed not to notice that we were taking a particularly risky road. And now I fear that we are well and truly stuck.

Then you ask how long we will be here and you look at me as if I'm supposed to have all the answers.

I wish I knew. What I do know is that I fear two things.

One: we just sit and sit and sit, too scared to take another step in case things deteriorate further. The sun will

... a green valley, where there were shadows, leaves shifting in sunlight, a stream that brimmed its banks

set and rise again tomorrow and blaze all day long so that we grow drier and drier.

Two: one of us leaves, in the hopeless hope of finding rescue, some way of salvaging the situation. Both of us know, though, that if that happens, we may never see each other again.

What to do?

Sometimes the best thing to do, for the time being, is simply to wait. Sometimes it is better not to talk and fret, not to try and fix anything, even if inside we are scared and anxious to see it all change for the better. We want, so badly, to be gone from this desert place and, preferably, back in that green, shaded valley.

You know and I know, though, that the only possible way is forward. There never truly is any going back and if we actually managed to reach 'before', we may find ourselves—if we are not careful—as no better than ghosts, haunting a place that has long since forgotten about us. Even if we found our way back to that green valley, autumn may have come, and the leaves fallen, the stream vanished under the rocks.

Dare we think about 'forward'? I don't know about you but I worry that I am too parched to stand, let alone take another step. We need to find water but we can't dig a well; we have no shovel except our bare hands and I am too tired to dig.

We can't walk to the mountains in this heat and, anyway, you can see as well as I can that they are as bare and brown as the place where we sit. No oasis shimmers in the middle distance; no heap of broken bricks hints at a ruined well within relatively easy reach.

To be honest, I know that you would have left earlier if you hadn't felt bad about abandoning me. I'm sorry about that, because it's too late now.

Thirsty.

Sometimes the best thing to do, for the time being, is simply to wait

It's strange how you can imagine things. Like now, sitting here, I imagine the tiniest of breezes beginning to blow. Looking up into the blank blue sky, I imagine I can see the thinnest haze of cloud. Of course that's impossible, in such bone dryness.

It's nice to imagine, though.

… still thirsty…

So you're imagining it too—the breeze, picking up a little now, and the cloud haze, thickening and starting to stretch across the sun.

… dare we actually hope?

Then comes the first definite breath of wind; then come the first spots of moisture; finally there comes a spattering of rain that rapidly builds to a drenching downpour. Burning skin is cooled; the thirsty ground quenched, and hollows in the rocks overflow with brand-new pools.

Why now? Why not before? And what about later?

Don't know—but we can enjoy it, now. We can drink deep, enjoy the water. It is pure gift, the heavens opening and giving freely, beyond expectation, beyond our wildest asking.

Is it enough to keep us going, as long as we need?

Don't know—but it may be. Enough for now, anyway, enough to give us the energy we need to stand up, together, and walk on, together, until we come to a safer place.

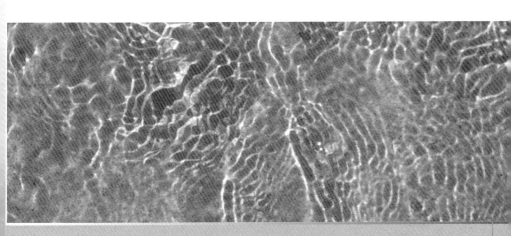

This space is for you to make your own notes.

Shallow water on a sunny day in Ireland

© Heather Fenton 2003

The waterless places: desert and spirituality

By definition a desert is an inhospitable place. In awe we watch television programmes about people who travel through such regions, wincing at the physical challenges they face and

author

Margaret Harvey, who lives in North Wales, is a retired priest and has been a regular contributor to *Quiet Spaces*.

wondering why on earth they do it. We worry about the effects of changing weather patterns on our water supplies, for we are used to being water-rich. The prophet Jeremiah describes the desert as 'a dry and dangerous land where no one lives and no one will even travel' (Jeremiah 2:6, GNB). If water is a symbol of life, both physical and spiritual, surely the desert, with its bleached carcasses and arid soil, is the very opposite.

But a strange thing happens in the Bible and in the later history of Christianity. The desert becomes the place of meeting with God. When the

If water is a
symbol of life,
both physical
and spiritual,
surely the
desert, with its
bleached
carcasses and
arid soil, is the
very opposite

prophet Hosea writes, out of the pain of unfaithfulness experienced in his own marriage, to call an unfaithful people back to God, it is to the desert that God calls them. 'I am going to take her into the desert again; there I will win her back with words of love' (Hosea 2:4). It was to the desert that Jesus went when he needed to sort out the implications of his baptism experience. In the fourth century those spiritual athletes that we call the Desert Fathers and Mothers went to the deserts of Egypt and the Middle East when they were challenged to radically live out the command to 'run with determination the race', ridding themselves of 'everything that gets in the way' (Hebrews 12:1).

Apart from actually living in a desert, something that won't be a life choice for most of us, the desert may still be part of our experience, in at least two ways.

The desert becomes the place of meeting with God

The practice of *lectio divina* has com to us through the monasticism th grew out of those desert experimen Through this slow, meditative readir of the Bible we are able to enter imaginatively so that the words are n confined to something that happene to other people in a different tim and place but become part of our ow spiritual journey too. 'Desert' has als become a symbol that describes ol own experience. We talk about 'dese times', being 'dry' spiritually, dese times of isolation or loneliness (bewilderment. Discovering the biblic desert can help when we find ourselve in what feels a 'real' desert place.

So journey with me into som of those places that are part of ol heritage as Christians. I suggest tha after you have read through the rest (this article quickly, you spend time wit each section. Read the section from th Bible slowly, out loud if you can do s without disturbing others. Read it a fe times. Pause at anything that catche your attention. Listen, look and wonde for as long as you like.

The desert of revelation: Exodus 3:1—4:17

The people of Israel are shaped b desert. The whole of the book of Exodu tells this story. These are not the sandy expanses of Egypt but a 'wilderness' of poor soil, of sparse vegetation and an equally sparse nomadic population, a place where water cannot be relied on and food, especially for people not used to these conditions, can seem non-existent. It is a thoroughly uncomfortable sort of place. But this becomes the place of revelation.

Moses is shepherding his father-in-law's sheep and goats in the wilderness/desert. Notice how the empty, hard, lonely spaces of the Sinai desert mirror the emptiness that Moses is experiencing. He has become aware of the need and suffering of the Hebrews—and when he tries to make a difference he discovers his inadequacy. He can't fix things; in fact he makes the situation even worse. After a privileged upbringing as an adopted member of the royal household, he has lost his position there as well as any standing he may have had among his own people (2:11–16).

Do you find that you can identify with Moses in any way? Do you long to change a situation but have to acknowledge your inability to make any impact?

This time of personal confusion and failure is the time of God's call and revelation. Notice God's persistent trust in Moses in spite of his incredulity. How does God use the desert? Its very emptiness draws Moses to investigate a bush that catches his eye. Maybe without the desert he would have

missed it. Elizabeth Barrett Browning wrote

Earth's crammed with heaven,
And every common bush afire with
God;
But only he who sees, takes off his
shoes,
The rest sit round it and pluck
blackberries.

ELIZABETH BARRETT BROWNING (1806–61)
SONNETS FROM THE PORTUGUESE

The desert, a growing place: Exodus 15:22—16:36

The desert is a place that enables us to exercise faith. Sir Francis Drake (1542–96) prayed, 'Lord God, when you call your servants to endeavour any great matter, grant us also to know that it is not the beginning, but the continuing of the same, until it be thoroughly finished, which yields the true glory.'

The Israelites soon find that being set free from slavery is very wonderful, but day to day 'continuing of the same' is altogether more problematical and can be rather scary. God gives them 40 years of what must have seemed rather pointless journeying. But it is far from pointless. During those years of rootlessness and uncertainty, they are given the chance to become a people and to learn to trust God. This passage is the beginning of that process. There isn't much trust in evidence. The people are full of grumbles and dissatisfaction. The desert is uncomfortable and demanding. There is little water and what there is tastes bitter. The scarcity of food wipes their memories clean of what God has done for them. Patiently God sets up for them a simple daily training course in faith. The manna is never 'money in the bank'. It arrives each day and there is enough for that day. But it can't be stockpiled or saved. Failure in trust simply results in a rotten, worm-infested heap.

Prayer for increased faith is often answered as we find ourselves having to use the scrap of faith we already possess. It is this exercise that makes faith muscles grow.

> Faith wasn't necessarily about effort—sometimes it involved sheer gift

If it all seems like very hard work, notice how God gave his grumbling people holidays. They didn't have to get up early every morning! One day in seven was a holy day, a holi-day. Some of them couldn't get their minds round the idea that God would countenance time off. They went off to gather manna as usual. I wonder if there was a certain amount of self-congratulation involved? But, as well as a lie-in, they missed out on discovering that faith wasn't necessarily about effort—sometimes it involved sheer gift.

The desert became such a precious growing place that, all these thousands of years later, we are still mining their findings.

The desert where God acts: Psalm 107

When the Old Testament writers wanted to remind their people of God's care and love for them as well as his power and awesomeness, they looked back to the desert, reminding them of the time when they had 'wandered in the trackless desert' and 'in their trouble they called to the Lord, and he saved them from their distress' (v. 6). Time brings clarity and enabled them to go to the heart of what was happening. The difficulties

they had grumbled about are put to one side and they are able to see patterns and meanings through the confusion. So, at another time of national turmoil, the prophet could write, 'When the Lord led his people through a hot, dry desert, they did not suffer from thirst. He made water come from a rock for them; he split the rock open, and water flowed out' (Isaiah 48:21). It all felt very different at the time!

Sometimes people who come to stay at our retreat house ask us how it came about. We tell them the story. I am always struck by how many times an important move forward has developed out of a time that could be described as 'desert'. Jesus compares such times to childbirth (see John 16:21). More mundanely, I think of the experience of following a

Deserts are places of wide horizons and large skies

complicated knitting pattern that had no accompanying picture. One simply had to go doggedly on, following the instructions with no idea of how it could turn into anything wearable. Gradually a pattern emerged—but I could make no sense of it at all at the time.

As you read the Psalm you may find that memories of your own desert times begin to surface. Don't feel you have to force them to make sense or to pretend they were wonderful at the time. Deserts are uncomfortable and challenging places. Hold them out anew to God.

Make yourself a quiet corner... and share it with others

Take a container of water, preferably something transparent like a glass jug, and place it in the centre of your table. As you put it down, thank God for Jesus:

Pour out some of the water and drink it. If you are with others, share it with them but make sure some remains in the jug.

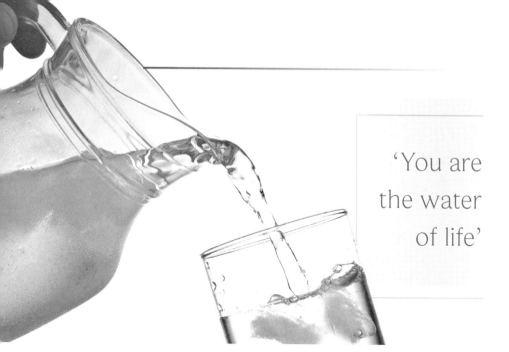

'You are
the water
of life'

Lord God, thank you for Jesus, who is the water of life. May we who drink of his living water be filled with his life and goodness.

Sprinkle a small amount of water around yourselves.

Lord God, thank you for Jesus, who is the water of life. May that living water flow out from us to those who are thirsty, that their thirst may be quenched too.

Take time to look at the water left.

Jesus was the one through whom all things were created and in whom all things hold together. The writer to the Colossians says: 'The Son is the image of the invisible God, the firstborn over all creation. For in him all things were created: things in heaven and on earth, visible and invisible, whether thrones or powers or rulers or authorities; all things have been created through him and for him. He is before all things, and in him all things hold together' (Colossians 1:15–17, NIV).

Lord God, thank you for Jesus, who is not only the water of life but the one through whom all things have their being.

Pour some of the water into a small bowl and draw a sign of the cross in it.

Read from Romans 6:4: 'We were therefore buried with him through baptism into death in order that, just as Christ was raised from the dead through the glory of the Father, we too may live a new life.'

Lord God, thank you for Jesus, who is not only the water of life and the one through whom all things have their being, but also the one who calls us through baptism to be united with him in his death and resurrection.

Pour some water into a measuring jug of the kind you may use for cooking.

The story of the woman at the well shows us someone coming on a regular trip to fetch some water. While she is there, she has an encounter with Jesus that will change her life. Jesus said to her: 'Everyone who drinks this water will be thirsty again, but whoever drinks the water I give them will never thirst. Indeed, the water I give them will become in them a spring of water springing up to eternal life' (John 4:13−14).

Lord Jesus, we thank you for showing yourself to us. You are the water of life, the one through whom all things come into being. Lord, give us your living water

and enable us to share this well of water with those whom we come across in our everyday lives.

Place your Bible on the table, open at Revelation 22.

John, in the book of Revelation, describes for us pictures of the City of God where Jesus is seen to reign supreme: 'The angel showed me the river of the water of life, as clear as crystal, flowing from the throne of God and of the Lamb down the middle of the great street of the city' (22:1−2a).

Lord Jesus, may we and all who taste your living water in this life be with you in that holy city, and hear you say to us 'Well done, good and faithful servant… Come and share your master's happiness' (Matthew 25:21).

You could leave these things in the quiet corner for a while, maybe adding some flowers if you have any.

an encounter with Jesus

TONY HORSFALL

Hope for the downcast

author

Tony Horsfall is a freelance trainer and retreat leader, living in Yorkshire. He has written a number of books, including *Rhythms of Grace* (BRF, 2012), *Working from a Place of Rest* (BRF, 2010) and *Mentoring for Spiritual Growth* (BRF, 2008), and he contributes to *New Daylight* Bible reading notes. For further information, see www.brfonline.org.uk.

The death of the Wales football manager Gary Speed in November 2011 shocked everyone, even those with no interest in football. The fact that it seems to have been related to depression enabled other men (especially sports people) to acknowledge that they also struggle with what Churchill called his 'black dog' and brought the subject of depression into open discussion.

It is said that one in four people in the UK will experience some form of the illness during their lifetime. I remember vividly in my teenage years watching my father struggle with depression after he was made redundant, and I have friends for whom depression has been a constant, if unwelcome, visitor throughout their lives. One of the reasons I love Psalm 42 is that it deals with this common human affliction, albeit from a slightly unusual angle— that of spiritual depression.

Spiritual depression occurs when we lose our sense of God's presence and experience a loss of enthusiasm for the disciplines that normally sustain our relationship with God, like prayer, Bible reading and fellowship. It is an extremely common problem in Christian discipleship, highlighted in 1965 with the publication of *Spiritual Depression, its causes and cures*, (Picking & Inglis, 1965), the substance of a series of sermons preached at Westminster Chapel, London, by the minister Dr Martyn Lloyd-Jones.

... what Churchill called his 'black dog'

The anonymous writer of Psalm 42 appears to have been a highly committed and talented believer, probably a temple singer or musician. The context suggests this person has been exiled from Jerusalem (perhaps to Babylon?) and can no longer take part in the communal worship as before (v. 4). He carries within him a deep sense of disappointment in God for allowing Jerusalem to fall to its enemies, and the taunts that God has deserted Israel exacerbate his melancholia (vv. 3, 10). A deep sadness engulfs him and he weeps constantly (v. 3). It seems as if God is to blame for his misfortune (v. 7); eventually his health begins to suffer (v. 10).

The opening verses of the Psalm are among the most well-known in scripture and capture the essence of his desperate longing: 'As the deer pants for streams of water, so my soul pants for you, O God. My soul thirsts for God, for the living God. When can I go and meet with God?' (vv. 1–2, NIV). The writer feels like a deer running for its life, harried and exhausted by the chase, desperate for refreshment and safety. Spiritually, he is parched and dry. He knows that only God can satisfy his soul, but how can that happen when he is far away from the promised land?

Then faith begins to rise within him; slowly and gradually light and truth dawn upon his troubled soul. The Psalm's chorus, repeated three times (42:5, 11 and 43:5) represents his fight back and the way in which his prayer is answered: 'Why are you downcast, O my soul? Why so disturbed within me? Put your hope in God, for I will yet praise him, my Saviour and my God.'

There are no magic formulas for lifting depression, and the fact that the psalmist has to listen to his own advice repeatedly suggests that relief is likely to come gradually, but the flow of the Psalm (which continues into Psalm 43) shows a growing hopefulness and a sufficient lifting of the gloomy cloud to hearten anyone battling with a similar malaise. What then can we learn from his struggle?

❖ Firstly, be honest. It is better not to pretend that things are better than they are. If you are downcast, admit it, at least to a trusted few. There is no shame in battling with depression, and we need not feel guilty because we feel overwhelmed or can't cope.

Thinkstockphotos

No one can help us if we hide our symptoms and mask our true feelings.

❖ Secondly, ask questions, especially of yourself. Why am I downcast? Is there a reason for my feelings? This is one of the key insights of Cognitive Behaviour Therapy. It helps us to see the connection between our thoughts and our feelings, and that wrong thinking leads to negative emotions and eventually depression. While not all depression has its source in a wrong belief system, spiritual depression often does, and it is worth exploring our thought patterns with a counsellor or wise friend. It is easy to see, for example, that if the psalmist was thinking God had been defeated, he would inevitably feel downcast. In fact God had not been defeated, and there was another explanation for the fall of Jerusalem: the discipline of God.

❖ Thirdly, have faith. It is easy to allow self-pity to overwhelm us and sometimes we have to take ourselves in hand and speak faith to our troubled souls. This was one factor that Lloyd-Jones emphasised: 'We must talk to ourselves, instead of allowing "ourselves" to talk to us. Most of your unhappiness in life is due to the fact that you are listening to yourself rather than talking to yourself.' Faith has to be exercised, and in dark times we must remind ourselves of the truth that God has given us and believe that we will again praise God. 'Weeping may stay for the night, but rejoicing comes in the morning' (Psalm 30:5).

❖ Fourthly, lean hard. The psalmist is connected to God in a deeply personal way. He speaks of 'my God' and 'my Saviour'. Here is a moment to remember that it is God's hold upon us that matters, not so much our hold upon him. He has taken hold of us and will never let us go, no matter how we feel. We are held in the grip of grace. We can lean our full weight upon his faithfulness, allowing him to take the strain, and trust that we will sing again (43:4).

Daybreak will come

This does not mean that recovery will be easy or quick, but it does mean there is hope. However dark it is now, daybreak will come and we will find once more the streams of living water.

Margaret's Space

Margaret Harvey is a retired priest in the Church in Wales. She has been running Coleg y Groes Retreat House. Margaret writes a regular column in *Quiet Spaces*.

Watery grumbles...

The village has been taken over by coils of blue. The water piping is being renewed. There are inconvenient excavations. Lanes are blocked, life disrupted. It is all taking a very long time.

It is raining *again*. No question of hose pipe bans in this part of the world.

Spring seems to have been put on hold.

Water is dripping through the ceiling in our house. We have to send for the plumber to discover where, among all the pipes in the loft, something has gone wrong.

One of my fellow students at theological college had been a nurse in a part of the world where the water supply was at best intermittent and often non-existent. 'You simply don't appreciate it,' she would say.

So thank you, Lord, for the blue coils which mean we have water available at the turn of a tap.

Thank you for the ingenuity and sheer hard work that has made this possible.

Thank you for baths and showers and washing machines and mop buckets.

Thank you for water to cook and drink and brush our teeth afterwards.

> Thank you Lord for the green grass, for the mountain waterfalls, for filling reservoirs

Thank you, Lord, for the green grass, for the mountain waterfalls, for filling reservoirs.

Thank you, Lord, for all this complicated array of plumbing that we take for granted and for the expertise of the person who understands it.

And the water of life…

Thank you, Lord, for the people who made the connections, who brought the living water a much greater and more dangerous distance than the blue plastic coils have to go.

Thank you, Lord, for the never-ending supply that you lavish on us for our own living and for sharing. 'Whoever is thirsty should come to me, and whoever believes in me should drink. As the scripture says, "Whoever believes in me, streams of life-giving water will pour out from his side"' (John 7:37, 38, GNB).

Thank you, Lord, for churches and networks, chat rooms and websites, meetings and study groups, Bibles and literature, songs and pictures; all the complex arrangement of 'plumbing' that makes the water of life available.

'Give thanks to the Lord... he satisfies those who are thirsty' (Psalm 107:1, 9).

Thank you, Lord, for the never-ending supply that you lavish on us

Psalm 107:1—8

(tune: French Carol)

Thank the Lord for he is gracious
And his love eternal stands
Let this be your song of worship
You who come from many lands
Rescued from the earth's four corners
Brought to safety by his hand.

Some were wandering in the desert
Homeless, searching for a way,
Overcome with thirst and hunger
Knowing they were far astray
When they cried for God to help them
From their trouble and dismay

Then he led them by a straight road—
Oh, with joy, his praises sing!
Led them to a place of safety—
Sing the love of God our King!
For he satisfies the thirsty
Fills the hungry with good things.

Living waters

author

Carol Jerman, who lives in
north Wales, walks with her
llamas and with the people
in a local group of churches,
where she is a Reader.

1.

*Draw us to the place, O God,
The place from which the living
waters flow;
The sanctuary of the Holy One
And that profound meeting place
Where he was pierced,
Where the Rock was smitten.*

*They flowed from your Son,
And they are flowing still,
Streams of living water
Enough for all.*

*Draw us to that meeting place,
O God,
The place of his piercing.*

*Our God and our Father,
Help us to abide in the place of
the cross,
And in your grace to know the
crucified Christ
From whom alone the living
waters flow.*

2.

*Father,
Help us always to remember that
the One from whom the living
waters flow
Said, 'I thirst.'
Create in us a deeper thirst for
righteousness.
Fill your Church with longing for
justice in the earth
And for the honour of your name
So that the waters may flow.*

3.

There is a tree that makes bitter
waters sweet;
O apply it to my heart, most holy
Lord.
I'm longing now for all that flows
from me to be like sweet, pure
water,
And I mourn because of the
brackish stuff,
Discoloured and bitter to those
around me
That still issues from me.
Help me, Father, so to abide in the
love of Christ
That this love springs consistently
from my life.

Help all those who trust in you,
O Christ,
To live in the good of all you have
bought for us, your Church.
There are so many things that can
make the waters bitter;
Pride and judgmental attitudes, lack
of compassion and lack of faith,
Self-importance and false humility,
insecurity and self-centredness,
Cowardice and ambition.
Lead us in the ways of the
Lamb who gave himself for our
redemption.

Forgive us, Lord, for all the times
when we have drunk of your clear,
flowing water,
And then turned and, trampling in
it, muddied it, making it unfit for
others to drink,
So that they have gone away, still
thirsty.
Forgive us, Lord, and teach us how
to worship you in Spirit and in
truth.

The Water of Life 49

4.

Lord,
It is as if the desert is encroaching.
Your Church grows thin,
The land, a wilderness.

Where is the garden of the Lord
From which the rivers flow
Into a thirsty land?
There is a bitter taste in our
mouths:
We have drunk from other streams,
Forgive us, Lord.

Only faith perceives the water from
the Rock
And only love can drink.
Cleanse our hearts of other things,
Lord Jesus.
Draw us again to yourself, so we
may drink,
And so the living water may spring
up in us
And flow out.

5.

So many faults remain in me
And in your Church,
So much sorrow and injustice in
the world.
Neither my prayers nor actions
seem to touch it
And I am weary,
And thirsty, thirsty for the
overflowing springs of the love of
God
And his everlasting grace.
This is a desert place to be.

O Lord, have mercy on us;

Christ have mercy.

Yet if everything should fail
And all of heaven and earth pass
away
Still you endure, Lord Jesus,
And that is enough;
Enough for me, enough for me.

O Father, keep us in your love;

Christ, keep us in your grace.

And in this quiet place where only
your love remains,
Your Spirit wells up
Like a small, bubbling spring,
Like the laughter of those who
delight in one another.

O Lord, have mercy on us;

Christ have mercy.

We give you thanks, O Lord,
That your loving kindness endures
for ever;
And we will rejoice in God who is
our Saviour,
In God, who alone is our Saviour.

6.

Lord Jesus, in your grace
Give us thirst
And the understanding to come to
you and drink.
Give us grace to follow the Lamb
wherever he goes
Assured that you will lead us to the
river of God,
Pure water of life as a gift.
Give us faith to trust
That you give your Spirit to those
who drink of you,
An inner spring of eternal life,
Fellowship with God in every
circumstance of life,
Gift beyond measure.

7.

There came a sudden beauty of
waters:
Shining rain fell, drenching me and
the ground,
And a sudden burst of sunlight
bathed everything in warmth and
brilliance.
I stood with upturned face,
knowing that I was in the middle of
a rainbow
That I could not see but that could
be seen by others.

And so I pray,
Lord, may your covenant promises
be seen in us.
May the work of your grace be
visible when we don't see it,
In all the ups and downs of life.
Help us to remain in the place of
the rainbow,
Washed and given light by your
grace,
Because of all your Son has done
for us.

But blessed is the one who trusts in the Lord, whose confidence is in him. They will be like a tree planted by the water that sends out its roots by the stream. It does not fear when heat comes; its leaves are always green. It has no worries in a year of drought and never fails to bear fruit.

JEREMIAH 17:7–8 (NIV)

My Space

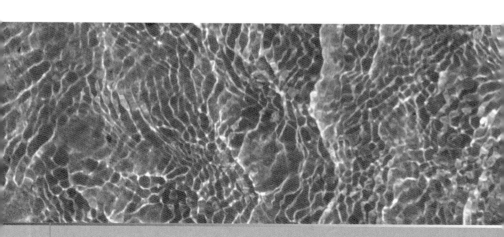

This space is for you to make your own notes.

Shallow water on a sunny day in Ireland
© Heather Fenton 2003

A poem about water

Here is a short poem I wrote about water. It was written for the children at the harvest festival when our theme was going to be water. Here in the UK water is something we easily take for granted. This poem may help us remember some of the places where water can be found. You may like to find ways of using it with a small group too.

Water

Water from the supermarket, water
from the spa,
Water from a shiny truck carried from
afar.

Water in an old tin can, water in a hose,
Water in a dirty hole where wild cattle
goes.

Water in a reservoir, water in the sea
Water in the food we eat and in our cup
of tea!

Water, sparkling, fast and free; water in
a sewer,
Water in a boggy place in somewhere
quite obscure!

Water in a little stream; water in the
river.
Water that has come from God, the
greatest ever giver!

Water in our story too; water in the font,
Water, living and eternal, all we'll ever
want!

Water in the universe; water in our story.
Water, water everywhere, says 'Now give
God the glory!'

©HEATHER FENTON 2006

article

Water and prayer Celtic style

The ancient Celtic peoples seemed attracted to water and believed that wet places offered access to the underworld. Indeed, because they thought of these places as where gods dwelt, they would sometimes leave hordes of treasure in such places. The fact that they did this has helped us to understand more of their wonderful design skills in early examples of what we now call Celtic art.

When Christians brought the gospel to the Celts on the western edges of Britain, they recognised the importance of bogs and wells and encouraged people to see that they could worship Jesus, who offered them living water, at such places. Thus the people kept their important sites but gave them a whole new meaning. As this new tradition took hold, such places became the focus of prayer and sometimes pilgrimage, and some can still be visited today.

Perhaps because of this, water is often associated with the places connected with Celtic saints. There is a well very near the place in Pembrokeshire, south-west Wales, where the Welsh patron saint David was born. His life begins with a thorough drenching as he was said to have been born in a thunderstorm. David's connection with water continued at his baptism when some of the water from the font is said to have splashed on to someone nearby, instantly healing them of blindness!

David, or Dewi as he may well have been known, grew up to be a strong and determined leader in spite of, or maybe because of, fierce opposition. He started a monastery not far from his birthplace and gave it a very strict rule. As well as saying that monks should plough without the use of animals, his monastic rule said that monks must drink only water and eat only bread with salt and herbs. They must have been among perhaps the earliest vegetarians as meat was definitely forbidden. His symbol, a leek, reminds us of this rule. When cooked, the leek is found to contain a great deal of water, another reminder of David.

Maybe because, generally speaking, they lived close to water, the Celts also used it for an opportunity for a rather demanding way of praying. Sometimes they would stand in cold water for hours on end, praying with their arms outstretched. It became known as a 'cross prayer' and must have been very demanding physically. I can just imagine David doing that, can't you?

> Such places became the focus of prayer and sometimes pilgrimage

David is sometimes known as 'Dewi Dŵr', the word *dŵr* being the Welsh word for 'water', so even his lifestyle became part of his memory. He is also famous for his last words, reputed to have been 'Keep the faith and do the little things well'. We may not be called to such excessive austerity but we are all called to keep the faith *and* do all those little things in a way that encourages us and others to live out the gospel in our own time and place.

Celtic places which have connections with water and which you could visit today include the well at St Non's, David's birthplace: see http://en.wikipedia.org/wiki/Chapel_of_St_Non. Another is the well at Holywell (see www.castlewales.com/winifred.html), which is connected with St Winefride. This saint, according to legend, had her head cut off by a would-be rapist but was healed by her uncle who was called Beuno. St Beuno, as he became known, became a saint of high standing in north Wales and is sometimes compared with David himself.

A psalm for singing:

Psalm 1
(tune: The Ash Grove)

O happy are those who reject evil counsel,
Who walk not with sinners or those who scorn right.
Instead they delight in obeying God's precepts,
They study and ponder his law day and night.
Like trees by the water that bear fruit and flourish
Whose leaves do not wither, they prosper and grow.
O happy are those who reject evil counsel,
Who walk not with sinners or those who scorn right.

But like winnowed chaff blown away by the strong wind,
The godless, when judged, are not able to stand.
They will not find room among those who are just, but
Like dry straw are blown from the face of the land.
But all who love God are protected and guided,
For God's way is life and apart from him, none.
O happy are those who reject evil counsel,
Their joy in the blessings that come from his hand.

©MARGARET HARVEY 2001

Like a tree planted by the waterside...

Psalm 1 (NIV)

Blessed is the one
who does not walk in step with the
wicked

author

Heather Fenton has spent
a number of years in parish
ministry as well as working
as an editor.

or stand in the way that sinners take
or sit in the company of mockers,
but whose delight is in the law of the
Lord,
and who meditates on his law day and
night.

That person is like a tree planted by
streams of water,
which yields its fruit in season
and whose leaf does not wither—
whatever they do prospers.

Not so the wicked!
They are like chaff
that the wind blows away.

Therefore the wicked will not stand in the judgment,
nor sinners in the assembly of the righteous.

For the Lord watches over the way of the righteous,
but the way of the wicked leads to destruction.

The wonder of the Psalms is at least in part because they help us to explore what it means to be a human being who is aware of God while struggling with being in the world with all its troubles and challenges. I just love this first psalm, which for me sets the scene for all that follows, helping us to think about how we may live out our lives faithfully in relationship to God. 'Blessed is the one… whose delight is in the law of the Lord,' the writer says of those who are seeking God and looking for his ways.

The picture the psalmist uses next is of a tree planted by the waterside. I am very fortunate in that there are two waterfalls very near my house, and so when I read this I usually think of them. As I live in a mountainous part of north Wales, naturally rowan trees spring to my mind. These slim trees have elegant leaves and they are at their most smart in the autumn when masses of red berries appear, shortly followed by birds who love to consume them. I am quite keen on rowan berries too as they make excellent jelly, which is particularly delicious with pork and has a wonderful deep red colour! They grow well in thin rocky soil but are often to be found above a ditch or, in my case, near the waterfalls.

However, where the palmists lived was nothing like here. He is probably much more accustomed to a landscape of low rainfall and dry scrub, so for him the picture is more vivid because it is more amazing. In such a landscape a tree would stand out regardless of the time of year and the presence, or absence, of bright berries. A tree planted by a stream would stand out in the dry landscape and draw attention to itself immediately, indicating the presence of water even if the observer could not see the stream. So it is with the person who is blessed; they stand out in the landscape long before the observer senses the presence of the water.

There is reason to go up to this tree, not just to get a closer look or to inspect it as a curiosity. Long before the water, the source of its prosperity, is seen, the fruit will stand out. There are no withered leaves here.

Embracing Du

author

Lynne E. Chandler spent her childhood in the Democratic Republic of the Congo and the United States. She lives with her family in Cairo, where she serves as the music director in the Anglican/Episcopal international church that her husband pastors. This is an extract from *Embracing Dusty Detours* (BRF, 2012). She has also written *Embracing a Concrete Desert* (BRF, 2010). See www.brfonline.org.uk for more information.

Water jugs

One evening, in the midst of a lively opening night at an art exhibition in central Cairo, I slowly squeezed my way through the throngs of an energetic crowd watching traditionally clad Nubian dancers and slipped into the calm of the final exhibition room. The volume levels outside had reached such a high pitch of celebration that I could picture my old dog, Pepsi, ten miles away standing at alert, ears twitching. I had lost my extravert husband somewhere along the way, but was happy to have a moment of respite. And then I saw it.

Across the room, a painting caught my eye and drew me in, like the rare meeting with a stranger whom you feel you have known for ever. Unlike its more vibrant neighbours, its colours were subtle and soothing—an invitation to reflection, something to ponder that

y Detours

was full of the earth and humanity and life. An ageless woman stood pouring fresh water into earthen jugs; her feet were bare and her arms were strong. The mud walls and floors of her home were spotless; a makeshift palm wood table held her three water jugs.

I was surprised to see that the picture had not been sold already. The price was very reasonable, but certainly beyond what we could justify at our time of life, with a child in university and another one drawing near to that age. Perhaps it was best. Besides, our walls were already full of meaningful art. It's one of three vices I share with my husband: art, books and caffeine. I wandered away, I wandered back, I became protective, I let go.

And then I saw it

Eventually I found my husband. He hadn't seen the final room yet, so I told him my favourite painting awaited him, and then I made myself scarce so that my eyes wouldn't give him any clues. He guessed it anyway. We both agreed there was no need for more art in our home, yet always more need to feed our souls. We planned to wait, to think rationally, to hope someone else would buy 'our' painting so that the decision

... like the rare meeting with a stranger whom you feel you have known for ever

would be made for us. The next morning I woke up with *Water jugs* on my mind, in desperate need to know if it had survived Opening Night. Christmas was around the corner and neither of us had anything on our lists yet. Then would come my birthday on the twelfth day of Christmas, then our anniversary at the end of that month... Stop. I let it go again.

The Egyptian artist was actually a friend of ours from church and had produced an incredible body of work for this exhibition, bringing to life a people group in Egypt rarely honoured, the Nubians. When the High Dam was built on the Nile River in Aswan in the 1970s, it displaced 60,000 people in Lower Nubia, and they continue to struggle to preserve their unique cultural identity. We now find many living around us in

Cairo, identifiable by their darker skin and often jovial personalities. When we first moved to Egypt, it took me a while to realise that 'lighter' skin was preferable in Cairo. One year, our daughter's school photo was lightened to such a ghostly hue that I had to meet with the photographer and have it redone, gently requesting no touch-ups, which surprised him.

Water in the desert country of Egypt is of vital importance, a treasured commodity. As the Nile River is the longest river in the world and flows some 4000 miles north, the question of who controls its water supply is often hotly disputed. Once, on an extended visit to central Africa, I remember

... an invitation to reflection, something to ponder that was full of the earth and humanity and life

walking almost a mile to a stream with some village women and children to help collect water, as the jungle home where I was staying had none. I slowed down traffic on the well-worn path up from the river more than once, as I was struggling to carry my heavy bucket without splashing out any of its precious contents. Several times, very young children politely slipped past me with jugs on their heads and big smiles on their faces, probably well amused by this crazy lady who didn't even know how to carry water. I became an expert at water conservation that summer, a skill that definitely comes in handy in Cairo when the taps run dry from burst water pipes in the ever-expanding, overloaded urban infrastructure.

I love the story of Jesus and his words to the woman at the well who asked him for a drink of water (John 4). When Jesus spoke of being the source of living water, he was saying it in a time and land where fresh water was scarce. Although the Nile is the main source of water for Egypt, fresh springs continue to sustain nomadic Bedouin, oasis communities and monastic life. My favourite monastery here in Egypt is St Anthony's, one of the oldest in the world. It is located several hours from Cairo, on a vast wilderness plain near

Thinkstockphotos

the Red Sea, wedged against dusty barren mountain ridges. It is surrounded by a tenth-century fortification wall, six feet thick and up to 40 feet high, and houses an active community of highly educated monks. Founded in the fourth century by the followers of the ascetic desert monk St Anthony (considered by many as the 'father of monasticism'), it is now a dynamic community, focused outward on its numerous pilgrims and on the life of the Coptic Orthodox Church here in Egypt.

> The years are timeless, the supply eternal

All my preconceptions about monastic life were thrown to the wind on our first visit, when our guide, an Egyptian monk from California, received a mobile phone call. I didn't even know there was coverage way out there in the middle of nowhere. He promptly pulled a slim mobile from a concealed pocket in his long, traditional, black monastic robe. Before his conversation had finished, another phone rang, and he pulled out a mobile from his other pocket, smiling sheepishly at our waiting group. Although there is an area preserved for withdrawal into quiet weeks of prayer and meditation, the monks we met were hard at work

coordinating retreats, leading tours and letting our children try out what they claim is 'the oldest elevator in the world' (with a pulley system still in place), which, for safety reasons, was once the only means of access into the monastery. An ancient mill, hand-tilled sustaining gardens and a restored chapel containing Crusader graffiti call you into another era. We bought honey made by their bees and drank from the Spring of St Anthony, a natural source of mountain water, flowing freely and linking us back in time.

As we left the monastery and drove back along the Red Sea toward home, I thought about the barren Sinai desert, just across the way, where God even provided water from a rock to sustain Moses and his quarrelling, thirsty followers (Exodus 17). Water is such an essential of life, yet I hardly give it a thought. I am usually consciously thankful for food when I eat, but rarely do I think to be thankful for water.

Fortunately, Paul-Gordon never gave up on the *Water jugs* painting. Because its cost was a stretch for us financially, we decided it would take the place of Christmas, birthday and anniversary gifts to each other that year. It would wear a rotating ribbon to commemorate each celebration that had funded its welcome. Paul-Gordon was out of town when the artist delivered the painting and spoke thoughtfully of what he had poured into it. I spoke of what it had said to me already. 'Timeless life-giving water' was the way he described it.

I couldn't possibly wait until Christmas to hang it up, and I found it the perfect location. A recently painted chocolate-brown wall set off its frame and blended it into its setting—our dining room. Yet I could see it perfectly from my favourite chair in the living room, like a window to look through, to ponder and wonder and feed from its message. The source of life-giving water poured forth when the foundations of the earth were laid. There is a spring that never will run dry—life, breath, the one who sustains, across the boundless stretches of time. The years are timeless, the supply eternal. May we drink fully from the water of life.

Life-giving water

A river of endless supply breaks forth,
From the timeless gift of creation.
With cleansing rain you wash the earth,
Eternal mystery of life.
Out of your heart flows living water,
Quenching thirst in a desert land.
From the fountain of life springs healing and strength,
Unsettled waters are calmed.
Enfold, restore, guide, renew,
Illumine the source of such mystery.
Care poured generously on the garden of life,
Unrestrained life-giving water.
Our days are full of your goodness, Lord:
Boundless, sustaining, eternal.

My Space

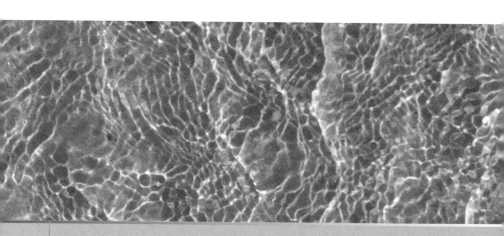

This space is for you to make your own notes.

Shallow water on a sunny day in Ireland
© Heather Fenton 2003

ANNE LE TISSIER

Jesus:
Name above all Names

author

Anne Le Tissier is a freelance writer and speaker, whose work aims to teach, encourage and equip Christian discipleship as well as engage with those on the fringes or even hostile to faith. Her book *Jesus: Name above all Names* (BRF, 2012) offers 32 Bible studies based on the names of Jesus.

Jesus: Light of the world

The prophet Isaiah foretold that God would send the light of his presence to his people (Isaiah 9:2; 42:6; 49:6) and, approximately 700 years later, Jesus declared in the Jerusalem temple, 'I am the light of the world. Whoever follows me will never walk in darkness, but will have the light of life' (John 8:12, NIV 1984). I wonder, however, if the analogy to light fails to inspire our relationship with Christ as readily as images of the counsellor or shepherd.

If so, then let's bear in mind that knowing Jesus as the light does not refer so much to the character whom we relate to as the atmosphere in which we live—energised and illuminated by his presence.

Jesus, the light of life

Light is fundamental for life. In fact, I vividly recall my biology teacher explaining, in her usual exuberant, passionate style, the 'fascinating' process of photosynthesis—the means by which plants obtain energy, and therefore life, from light.

We were all given two glass jam jars, blotting paper and two broad beans.

Inserting the beans into the jars between the rolled-up paper and glass, we added a dash of water before placing one jar on a sunny windowsill and the other in a dark cupboard. (Apologies if I fail

The 'fascinating' process of photosynthesis

to exude the same excitement as my teacher!)

A few lessons later, we noted how the beans on the windowsill grew strong green shoots and creamy roots, then flowered and produced further seed. The beans left in the dark, however, struggled to produce only a few pallid, emaciated spindles before dying without even flowering. That image has stuck with me as I consider life lived in the light of Christ.

Jesus didn't intend for us to struggle in our spiritual development, but came so that we might experience the power and vitality of his life. To do so, we need to keep ourselves in the light of his presence, just as beans need to be kept in the sunlight in order to grow and seed.

Paul taught further on this subject when he encouraged the Ephesians to 'live as children of light (for the fruit of the light consists in all goodness, righteousness and truth)' (Ephesians 5:8–9). We can't expect to grow or enjoy a fruitful spiritual life, to experience the ever-increasing transformation into his likeness (2 Corinthians 3:18) or the full measure of Christ within (Ephesians 4:13), unless we remain in the presence of his light and seek to live by his ways.

I know fairly quickly when I've taken myself outside the light of his presence, be that through wilful rebellion or the conviction of unintentional sin, and it's a horrid place to be. When I'm done with exhausting myself by trying to justify my behaviour, I'm left with the cold, dark misery of a barren prayer life, uninspired work, tetchy attitudes toward others, lack of fulfilment or an oppressive burden haranguing my emotions—that which we call condemnation.

There are times when I actually sit and fester in this dark place of the soul—unwilling to let go of my self-satisfying traits or too proud to confess that I've been wrong. But while coming back into the light of Christ's presence (through sincere, heartfelt confession) is a humbling, soul-searching, even sacrificial experience, it is always accompanied by Christ's unconditional love, relief from oppressive guilt, the

> There are times when I actually sit and fester in this dark place of the soul

The power and vitality of his life

washing of forgiveness and the healing balm of grace.

'Whoever lives by the truth comes into the light' (John 3:21). We each have a choice to accept the truth that Jesus is the Messiah and, as we do so, the divine light of his life infuses eternal life to our spirits. But we also have a choice then to live by that truth—placing ourselves, as it were, on the sunny windowsill rather than remaining in the cupboard, living our lives in the light of Christ's presence instead of the ways of darkness. It's only as we put his teaching into practice that the full potential of Christ's vitality can energise, empower and bear fruit, in and through our lives.

Jesus, the light to live by

Light is aptly defined in my dictionary as 'the medium of illumination that makes sight possible'.

If you've ever been caught doing something wrong, you'll know how you wished you could have turned off the light. But if you ever try cleaning out a dusty, dirty attic strewn with spiders' webs and mouse droppings, you'll appreciate the help of an electric bulb. If you ever try to study from a comprehensive textbook, you'll appreciate a decent desk lamp. If you ever try walking in the dark along an isolated country lane, you'll appreciate the guidance of a torch. And if you ever feel the gut-wrenching fear of darkness, you'll appreciate the comfort of a nightlight.

Similarly, the world in which we live is steeped in spiritual darkness that enshrouds our lives with sin, confusion, lack of direction, hopelessness, fear, isolation and so on. But Jesus, the light of the world, brings both life and illumination into this barren shadow of spiritual death—light that imparts righteousness, truth, clarity, revelation, guidance, direction, hope, comfort and reassurance. While the interaction of light with the retina in the eye enables

You'll appreciate the help of an electric bulb

us to see, so the contact of Christ's light with our souls enlightens the eyes of our hearts (Ephesians 1:17–18).

We can choose to stumble around in the darkness relying on our limited opinions, abilities and physical senses to do what we feel is right, to fathom the infinite depths of scripture, to choose what we think is best for our lives and seek solace or satisfaction in the company of the fickle, temporary attractions of the world. But consider how that wastes the potential resources made available to us in the light of Christ's presence.

If we take the time to pause—to pray, to listen, to read God's word—the presence of Christ's light will surely guide the way far better than our own intuition. Furthermore, it will comfort us when the going gets tough, encouraging us to persevere rather than give up.

I hope this brief reflection on Christ as the light of the world is helpful, but we can't quite leave it there, for as much as we are empowered and led by his light, we also have a responsibility to share it with others.

You are the light of the world

Jesus described John the Baptist as a lamp that gave light (John 5:35), born

The divine light of his life infuses eternal life to our spirits

into his generation for the unique purpose of pointing others to Jesus and revealing who Jesus was. We too are lamps, filled with the light of the life of Christ by his Holy Spirit so that others may see and recognise him for themselves.

This astounding truth begs the question, what are we doing with our lamps? If we're seeking to live in the light of Christ's presence, our lamps will indeed be bright as they reflect his glory—but with whom are we sharing that light? Are we trying to hide our lamps within our home, church and circle of Christian friends, or beneath a cloak of compromise? Or are we lamps with legs—taking Christ's light into the world to shine before others, 'that they may see [our] good deeds and praise [our] Father in heaven' (Matthew 5:16)?

Our lamp will shine Christ's light into the spiritual darkness where we live, work and socialise; its purity will contrast with the impurity of sinful behaviour; its truth will counter deceit; its comfort will reassure those in despair; its hue of grace will offer hope to a culture striving for love, acceptance and success. Moreover, it will reveal the person of Jesus.

We cannot force people to accept him; in fact, some will prefer the life lived in darkness (John 3:19). Others, however, who recognise our fulfilment and purpose in life, our genuine sincerity, integrity and love and our peace in difficult circumstances, and are attracted by the confidence we have for today and for the future, might well perceive Christ's light in the darkness and ask us the question, 'What is it that's different about you?'

Each one of us is unique. We all have different experiences, upbringings, characters, genes, skills, interests and relationships. But if we've accepted Jesus as Lord, we all share the same life-giving light. Let's determine to remain in that light and so let it shine brightly in our particular place in the world.

Take it further

Reflect

What challenges you?

❖ Have you accepted Jesus as your personal Saviour and Lord? If so, would you consider that you've grown spiritually over the last six months—that your relationship with Jesus has deepened and your submission to his ways has been refined?

❖ Are you prone to racing into decisions, responsibilities or simply the routine of your day without first focusing on Jesus and what he might want to say or do?

❖ How obvious and accessible is the lamp of your life to people who've yet to know Jesus themselves?

Pray

Lord Jesus, I'm reminded that you didn't merely describe yourself as the light, but you possess the very qualities of light that I need, to grow spiritually, to follow your ways and your paths, and to reveal you to other people. Please show me the ways by which I step into the shadows, thereby diminishing the brightness of your life in me.

We all share the same life-giving light

Read

John 1:1–13; 8:12–30; Ephesians 4:17–5:21; 1 John 1:5–10

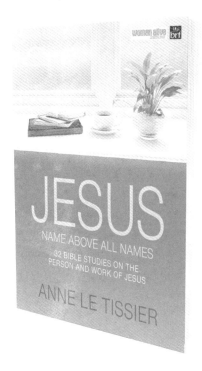

And at the end of the year...

author

Heather Fenton has been editor of *Quiet Spaces* since 2009.

As my time as editor of *Quiet Spaces* comes to an end, I have taken a moment to reflect on the past and look to the future during a period when there are a number of things changing in my own life. For me, particularly during the period of Advent, there is a time to look ahead and rejoice at what is to come, even if I know little of what it may hold. This is because at the end of all ends, there is Jesus. At Advent, the beginning of the Christian year, we focus our looking for his coming again with power and great glory by taking these four weeks to acknowledge him as Lord of all time and eternity, before celebrating his coming into the world as a small and vulnerable human being.

Thinkstockphotos

The second coming of Christ, for which we look, is anticipated in the strange imagery of the book of Revelation, where the writer has to use word pictures to describe what he wants to say. At the beginning of chapter 22, the angel shows John 'the river of the water of life, as clear as crystal, flowing from the throne of God and of the Lamb…' and 'on each side of the river stood the tree of life… and the leaves of the tree were for the healing of the nations' (Revelation 22:1–2, NIV). This has some of the same imagery as Psalm 1, about which I have written on pages 59–60, and of course echoes Jesus when he says, 'Let everyone who is thirsty come to me and drink. Whoever believes in me, as the scripture has said, rivers of living water will flow out from within them' (John 7:37).

The psalmist says that the godly person will be 'like a tree planted by streams of water' (Psalm 1:3). For the psalmist this was an individual, godly person who would prosper because he (or she) was set beside the water which gave them life. Here in Revelation we have the same sort of image but on a much, much larger scale. The water is clearly flowing from 'the Lamb', an image of Jesus, flowing through the midst of the holy city in which God dwells. The water near the trees enables them to bring forth leaves 'for the healing of the nations' (Revelation 22:2). Those who are permitted to enter the city will see the Lamb of God. Thus the individual is seen to be part of the whole people of God, part of the big story and the transformation to which John looks forward as he records his strange visions.

So we who thirst for Christ's living water in our own lives can also thirst for the coming of his kingdom. I hope *Quiet Spaces* under my editorship has made a contribution towards this for you, and so I leave you with an extract from the recently published book *Encircling the Christian Year* by Barbara Mosse (BRF, 2012). The author uses the response which I call to mind now: 'Lord of the ages, deepen our thirst for the coming of your kingdom.' Amen to that!

We can also thirst for the coming of his kingdom

Barbara Mosse
Foreword by Jane Williams

Encircling
the Christian Year

Liturgies and reflections
for the seasons of the Church

The Second Sunday of Advent

Opening prayer

Lord God, you come to us from all eternity with gifts of wisdom and love. May we worship you in awe and wonder, and may the prophetic voices of old find fresh resonance in our hearts, this Advent-time and always. Amen

Reading

A shoot shall come out from the stock of Jesse, and a branch shall grow out of his roots. The spirit of the Lord shall rest upon him, the spirit of wisdom and understanding, the spirit of counsel and might, the spirit of knowledge and the fear of the Lord. His delight shall be in the fear of the Lord. He shall not judge by what his eyes see, or decide by what his ears hear; but with righteousness he shall judge the poor, and decide with equity for the meek of the earth.
ISAIAH 11:1–4A, NRSV
(READ ALSO VV. 4B–10)

Reflection

*When Adam's flesh and Adam's bone
Sits at Cair Paravel in throne,
The evil time will be over and done.*

So goes the old prophecy in C.S. Lewis' *The Lion, the Witch and the Wardrobe*, in which the land of Narnia is held fast in the frozen grip of winter by the evil White Witch. There is a resonance here of the prophetic voice of Isaiah, echoing down to us through the corridors of history. So familiar are his words likely to be to us that we automatically hear them as a foretelling of the coming of Christ. Indeed, that is what they are—articulating our deep desire for a society of equity, peace and justice—but the prophecy also related directly to the society of the writer's own time,

... a foretelling of the coming of Christ

expressing a longing for a new and ideal Davidic king who would right present wrongs and usher in a new reign of peace and prosperity.

And this is not all, for such a reign would also usher in the reign of God through all creation: a new order would be initiated, where predators and prey would happily coexist. Such harmony may be difficult to imagine but God calls us all to hope and trust and to work with him for the coming of his kingdom.

Short silence

Bidding prayers

Let us pray to God, the wisdom of the ages, who comes to us from beyond the boundaries of time and space.

Son of David, branch of Jesse: open our hearts to your reign of justice and gentle love:
Lord of the ages, deepen our thirst for the coming of your kingdom.

Son of David, branch of Jesse: guide the leaders of the nations with your spirit of knowledge and wisdom:
Lord of the ages, deepen our thirst for the coming of your kingdom.

Son of David, branch of Jesse: open our ears to the cries of the poor, and the need for justice in our society:
Lord of the ages, deepen our thirst for the coming of your kingdom.

Son of David, branch of Jesse: may we long for that day when all creation is healed and renewed, and the earth is full of the knowledge of the Lord:
Lord of the ages, deepen our thirst for the coming of your kingdom.

Collect

Almighty God,
in times of old you spoke through the prophets,
infusing their words with the hidden presence of the Christ to come;
may our hearts be attuned to your prophetic voice today,
and may your gifts of grace and discernment
reveal to us the hidden Christ,
veiled within the darkness and light of our world.
In Jesus' name we pray.
Amen

Subscriptions to Quiet Spaces—new look, content and price

Quiet Spaces is published three times a year, in May, September and January. To take out a subscription, please complete this form, indicating the month in which you would like your subscription to begin.

☐ I would like to take out a subscription myself

Name _____

Address_____

Postcode_____ Telephone Number _____

Email_____

☐ Please do not send me further information about BRF publications.

☐ I would like to give a gift subscription (please complete your name and address
above and details of the person you want to give a subscription to below)

Gift subscription name _____

Gift subscription address _____

_____

_____Postcode_____

Please send beginning with the May 13 / Sep 13 / Jan 14 issue: (delete as applicable)

(please tick box)	UK	SURFACE	AIRMAIL
Quiet Spaces	☐ £15.00	☐ £17.10	☐ £20.25

Please complete the payment details below and send this coupon, with payment to: BRF, 15 The Chambers, Vineyard, Abingdon OX14 3FE.

Method: ☐ Cheque (payable to BRF) ☐ Mastercard ☐ Visa ☐ Maestro

Card no. ☐☐☐☐ ☐☐☐☐ ☐☐☐☐ ☐☐☐☐ ☐☐☐☐ ☐☐☐☐

Valid from ☐☐☐☐ Expires ☐☐☐☐ Issue no. of Maestro card ☐☐☐

Security Code ☐☐☐

Signature _____ Date ____ / ____ / ____

All orders must be accompanied by the appropriate payment.

BRF is a Registered Charity   PROMO REF: QSLIFE

To order *Quiet Spaces* or other BRF publications mentioned in this journal, visit your local Christian bookshop or go to BRF's website www.brfonline.org.uk.

Quiet Spaces is relaunched!

ISBN 978 0 85746 095 0 (May–August 2013 issue)
£4.00 per issue

Come on a journey with the new-look *Quiet Spaces*… From May 2013 *Quiet Spaces* will take a different shape, similar to our Bible reading notes in format and length while retaining its distinctive focus on prayer and spirituality—and all for less than its current price!

* Contains four months' worth of material

* Fortnightly sections including prayers, liturgy, meditation, creative ideas and Bible reflection

* Draws on a broad range of spiritual traditions

* Provides structure but accommodates flexible use

* Companion to our Bible reading notes

Edited by Sally Smith
Contributors in the May–August 2013 issue:

Sally Smith, Tony Horsfall, Helen Jaeger, Andrea Skevington, Daniel Muñoz, Claire Musters, Sally Welch, Cavan Wood

'*Quiet Spaces* provides exactly the kind of material I look for to resource my own walk with God. It is Bible-based but reaches out into the life of faith as lived by God's people down the centuries. It is informative and stimulating for the mind but warms the heart and can be personally applied, helping me to hear God's voice today. Further, it engages with real life, and provides workable ideas for use with others. The variety of contributors gives a freshness of perspective and groundedness that I appreciate. I warmly commend it to all who want to live deeply with God.'
Tony Horsfall

Available from your local Christian bookshop or, in case of difficulty, from BRF **www.brfonline.org.uk** 01865 319700

'The Water of Life' is the theme of this issue of *Quiet Spaces*. One of our
contributors is Naomi Starkey, the previous editor, who writes about
'Looking for Living Water'. Tom O'Loughlin explores the theme of
'The Water of Life' and Katharine Smith looks at the story of the
woman at the well in John 4.

'Searching for living water: pilgrimage, wells and sacred space' is the
title of Andrew Jones's contribution, while in contrast Margaret Harvey
writes about 'The waterless places: desert and spirituality'. Margaret
also has her regular column and Tony Horsfall, who has been a
long-term contributor to *Quiet Spaces* as well as being a regular
columnist, offers hope for the downcast. Finally, Carol Jerman
has written some prayers to fit in with our theme.

A wonderful source for meditation and prayer...

SISTER FRANCES DOMINICA, FOUNDER AND TRUSTEE HELEN & DOUGLAS HOUSE

Let those who risk taking 'time out' to read *Quiet Spaces* be
filled with the wonder, awe and beauty of what God presents
to them each day.

THE REVD CANON DAVID ADAM

www.quietspaces.org.uk

978-1-84101-874-4

UK £4.99

9 781841 018744

visit the **brf** website at www.brf.org.uk

Photograph: Yarygin/Shutterstock.com   Design: Louise Blackmore